MW01355632

b

Teaching Elephants to Talk

A Crash-Course in Campaign Communications

Matt Lewis

Published by The Campaign Leadership Company
Alexandria, VA

c

ISBN 1-59196-838-0

Printed in US by InstantPublisher.com

Contents

Dedication

In Memory of Marvin "Tex" Lewis

Acknowledgments

This book could not have been written without the help of some tremendous friends.

Morton Blackwell and everyone associated with The Leadership Institute have provided me with a tremendous foundational knowledge of politics. Their friendship and mentoring is greatly appreciated.

Numerous Republican leaders took the time to sit down with me as I was preparing this book. The list includes Lyn Nofziger, Ralph Reed, Joe Gaylord, and many others. Paul Wilson and Dan Hazelwood (both giants in the political consulting business) have both taught me a tremendous amount about politics and communications.

The beautiful and talented Erin DeLullo has been a blessing to me personally, as well as a tireless promoter of my political career. She gives me daily inspiration.

Tygh Bailes has been a loyal friend who was an inspiration to me as I wrote this book. His friendship proves that it *is* possible to have a trusted friend in Washington.

Jennifer Hoff, a communications expert in her own right, was a tremendous help in all facets of writing this book, including brainstorming ideas. She assisted in research and development of this book from the very beginning. This book is much better for her motivational intellectual support on a regular basis.

The entire Duane Sand for Congress Team provided friendship, laughs and advice while I worked on this book.

Alex Mooney, who gave me my first job in politics, deserves thanks for taking a chance on a kid who couldn't work a fax machine.

Thanks to my mother, Hope Lewis, for insisting that I "be somebody" when I grow up. Also, thank you mom for proofreading the final version.

The most important acknowledgement I make is to my father, Marvin "Tex" Lewis, who died while I was writing this book. He is the reason I first became interested in politics. None of the things I have accomplished, or will accomplish, would be possible without the guidance and love he showed me.

INTRODUCTION

Why I Wrote This Book

Ronald Reagan is my hero.

With his election in 1980, we finally had a president who was right on the issues – **and** knew how to communicate! His ability to inspire brought America back from the lethargy of the Jimmy Carter years. Like many Americans who came of age in the 1980s, I will always have a special place in my heart for "The Great Communicator."

As the 1990s began, another gifted communicator named Bill Clinton won two elections – sadly, for the other side. His mastery of public relations skills allowed him to defeat opponents who would have been better for America. For eight years I watched frustrated Republicans try to *prove* Clinton was a bad guy.

Many Republicans *still* don't understand that it was Clinton's mastery of public relations techniques that kept him high in the public-opinion polls. (Rumor has it that after the 1994 elections, President Clinton studied videotapes of Ronald Reagan in order to be a more effective communicator.)

Regardless of which political party is in power at any given moment, the truth is that you and I can never afford to rest on our laurels. In order to change America for the long run, conservatives must study how to effectively communicate *our* conservative message.

I've spent several years studying great communicators like Ronald Reagan and Bill Clinton (I don't like Clinton's politics, but you can't deny he's a good communicator). And, I've included as many of their techniques as I could into this book for you to learn from.

The lessons this book teaches will work for you as they did for me. Feel free to underline any thought that helps you. Keep this book handy. Review it often. With the right tools, I know you can help make America an even greater nation. I'm already excited about what you can accomplish!

Read on.

CHAPTER ONE

The Liberal Media

Why You Can't Afford to Ignore Them

Conservatives who believe they simply cannot work with the press ought not to be surprised when the press ignores them.
L. Brent Bozell, III

Before we get started, we should address something right away....

You see, no book designed to teach conservatives how to communicate could ignore the topic of the "liberal media."

The topic permeates our society. Shelves of books have been written about it.

Unlike those books, I won't attempt to uncover the underlying reasons for liberal media bias. Nor will I seek to prove to you the media are liberal. Rather, the purpose of this book is to help you succeed – regardless of the obstacles.

I've never understood conservatives who blame the liberal media for all their ills. Conservatives are "rugged individualists." If we find a problem, we fix it. That's what this book is about. It's about helping you figure out how to get your message out – no matter what the obstacles.

Sure, some reporters are biased. That will be the case in any state you work. So it's up to you to find the reporters that you *can* work with – and develop a relationship with them. As former reporter Dennis Staufer writes in his book, *Mediasmart*, "One of the first and most effective ways to influence a story is often overlooked: Choose who tells it. In many situations, *you can pick the reporter*."

I can personally attest to the fact the media are liberal. But, as reporter, turned author, Bernard Goldberg points out in his book, *Bias,* there is no vast left-wing conspiracy. Reporters don't wake up in the morning and ask, "How can I get those conservatives today?" Their bias isn't intentional. It's just a fact that most reporters come from a liberal worldview.

While there is a case to be made that the media are liberal, still, too many conservatives use the liberal media as an excuse. As Republican publicist Bill Kristol told the *New Yorker*, "…The whole thing (the liberal media) was often used as an excuse by conservatives for conservative failures." He was right.

I've run campaigns ranging from School Board to U.S. Congress, in states ranging from Maryland to North Dakota. I've also worked professionally to train candidates across America how to run for public office. I've had my share of run-ins with biased reporters. But I've also noticed that the candidates who *continually* receive bad press all have one thing in common: They all ignored the principles this book teaches.

Let me give you a hypothetical example: Two politicians announced their candidacy on the same day. The conservative candidate held his press conference in a fancy hotel. The liberal candidate held her announcement in front of a school – reading to children (a staged photo-op). Which candidate do you think got the best story written about them?

If you were a reporter or photographer, which announcement would you cover? Every single one of us (if we're being honest) would cover the candidate in front of the school. Yet, predictably, our hypothetical conservative candidate probably *believed* his announcement wasn't covered because of the "liberal media."

If you believe the media are intrinsically liberal – and that no matter what you do, you can't get good press – then you won't. It becomes a self-fulfilling prophesy.

Lesson Learned: It's up to you to make your campaign interesting.

The Making of a Cowboy

Former Reagan press secretary, Lyn Nofziger, faced an interesting situation while working for Reagan's gubernatorial bid in the 1960s. The media were going to visit the Reagan's ranch to conduct an interview. Much to Nofziger's chagrin, the future president came out of his ranch dressed in riding garb, including British riding boots.

Nofziger, thinking like a reporter, (he had been one before joining the campaign) sent the future president back inside to put on jeans, a flannel shirt, and a cowboy hat. That interview helped introduce Ronald Reagan to voters as a regular guy – and the rest is history. Because of his natural charm, his top-notch staff, and the fact that he practiced how to communicate, the "liberal media" could never paint Ronald Reagan as a *mean* conservative.

Lesson Learned: You <u>can</u> get good press if you look for the media angle in everything you do. (If the liberal media were omnipotent, we wouldn't still be calling Ronald Reagan, "The Great Communicator".)

Your "Inner Circle"

Sure, President Reagan was a naturally gifted speaker who was by nature positive and optimistic. But he was also smart enough to surround himself with staff who understood public relations. You should, too.

As Bill Press wrote in *Spin This!:*

> *Think of George W. Bush, say thank you to Karl Rove. See John McCain's success, look for John Weaver and Mike Murphy standing nearby. Bill Clinton? James Carville, George Stephanopoulos and Paul Begala. For Father Bush, gun slinger James Baker. And so it goes: Ronald Reagan's Michael Deaver, Jimmy Carter's Jody Powell and Hamilton Jordan, Nixon's Murray Chotiner and FDR's Louis Howe, among others.*

Lesson Learned: Surround yourself with good staff. They will make you look good.

Study How to Communicate

According to his aides, even after being elected president, Ronald Reagan continued to *study* how to be good communicator. If The Great Communicator had to practice, then what does that say about the need for the rest of us to study and practice communication skills?

By choosing to read this book, you've already demonstrated that you're the kind of person who is willing to study how to be a better communicator. I'm excited for you already!

Lesson Learned: You and I need to study – and practice – how to be great communicators.

Chapter One Lessons

The Liberal Media

Why You Can't Afford to Ignore Them

- The media is certainly liberal, but too often, conservatives use the liberal media as an excuse for getting poor media coverage.
- Some reporters are biased. It's up to you to find the reporters *you* can work with.
- It's up to you to make your campaign interesting.
- You and I need to study how to be great communicators.
- Surround yourself with good staff. They make you look good.

CHAPTER TWO

The Basics
Your Crash-Course in Public Relations

The average reporter is lazy, as the rest of us are, and sufficiently harassed by deadlines..."

-Lee Atwater

There are two important reasons your campaign *must* seek media attention: credibility and cost.

CREDIBILITY - *Earned media lends credibility to your campaign.* Voters (and consumers) rightly judge paid media more skeptically than earned media. *Many voters and consumers have grown cynical and view paid media as propaganda.*

Some businesses have caught on to this trend. Many now run newspaper or magazine ads meant to deceive readers into *believing* the ads are legitimate news stories.

Businesses realize that if an "unbiased" third party gives your product a good review, it carries more weight than self promotion. It's for this reason that most public speakers have someone else introduce them before speaking. Having someone trustworthy introduce you as an "expert" lends credibility to your speech.

COST - *The second reason to seek earned media attention for your campaign is simply becuase it's free.* Campaigns cost a lot of money. TV, radio, and voter mail are all expensive. Earned media allows you to get your name and message in front of the voters...for free.

Creativity Counts

To become good at public relations, start looking for the media angle in *everything* you do. This requires a conscious effort to be more creative and to pay closer attention to detail.

Your campaign could be either boring *or* interesting (depending on how you "sell" it). Think like a marketer. A good marketer will tell you that just because you have the best "product" doesn't mean you're going to survive in the marketplace.

In the 1980s Beta and VHS were competing to become the dominant producer of video cassette recorders. Beta made a better VCR, but VHS did a better job of marketing them. By 1990, nearly everyone had a VHS.

Lesson Learned: Having the best product isn't where it's at. You have to be able to sell your product.

It's just as true in politics. Just being *right* on the issues isn't enough to guarantee victory. Being right is just the beginning. The conservative movement has the best "products" (lower taxes and a strong national defense are very good products). But the hard part is being able to "sell" our ideas.

A friend of mine is an expert on marketing. He told me this story about a campaign he was working on:

The incumbent opponent was constantly vacationing at the beach. My friend's campaign wisely decided to make an issue out of this (after all, would you keep your job if you were constantly on vacation?).

But instead of holding a boring press conference to denounce the incumbent, my friend's campaign did this: They unloaded a dump truck full of sand on the incumbent's parking spot. And to really stress their point, they added a beach ball, an umbrella, and a podium.

Just as reporters were arriving, my friend's candidate steps to the mic and says, "If my opponent insists on spending all of his time at the beach, I thought I'd bring the beach to him!"

See how showing it is more interesting than just saying it? Imagine how much more interesting it is for a photographer or cameraman to cover the story!

On the Duane Sand for Congress race in North Dakota, we had excellent commercials, but were running low on money to get them on TV (we couldn't afford to get them up as early as we wanted to).

Our solution: Hold a contest to let voters pick which ad was their favorite. By thinking outside the box, we got folks to view our TV ads on our website. It didn't cost us a dime. And because it was a *creative* and new idea, we also got earned media out of it. Here's how *The Hill* reported it:

North Dakota's 'Special Guy'

Both candidates have winning qualities, but North Dakotans seem to favor a "special guy" in an ongoing and unusual election.

Last Thursday, North Dakota residents began voting on two separate ads for Republican House candidate Duane Sand, and, so far, "Special Guy," an ad focusing on Sand's career as a lieutenant commander in the Navy, is leading in the polls.

Sand's campaign hopes the online election-before-the-election gets voters more involved in the retired naval officer's race to unseat Rep. Earl Pomeroy (D).

"We think that the very first ad sets the tone for the entire campaign," said Matt Lewis,

campaign manager for the Republican contender. "Apart from that, we give folks the chance to be activists by simply using their keyboards."

The "Special Guy" ad has a substantial lead — 64 percent to 36 percent — over "Jobs," an ad that portrays Sand as a small-business owner who creates job.

Both ads are narrated by Sand's wife, Holly.

"She spoke at the state Republican convention and knocked the socks off of everybody," Lewis explained. "Holly is extremely charismatic and unquestionably better-looking than Duane."...

By being creative, we were able to spread the message that Duane Sand is a veteran who created jobs. And best of all, we were able to spread that message for free. You can do the same sort of things in your campaign…all it takes is creativity.

Timing is *Everything*

Creativity *is* vital. But a creative idea at the wrong time *still* won't work.

Let's say your campaign wants to talk about taxes. Even if you dress up in Colonial garb and reenact the Boston Tea Party, your event will probably fail if you hold it in January or August.

But suppose you decide to hold that press event on April 15 on a public sidewalk in front of the post office. In politics, that's called "riding the wave." The wave is what the media is going to cover with, or without you. The media will always do stories about taxes on April 15. It's an easy story for them to do.

Every year, local TV news stations show lines of people trying to mail their returns before midnight on April 15. That's because (like you and me) the average reporter is lazy. They know that an easy human-interest story every year is to talk about people filing their tax returns at the last minute. You might as well take advantage of their laziness and get some good press for your campaign at the same time.

Here's an example of *riding the wave* from that same campaign:

Candidates criticize lawmakers for spending

(Excerpted from the *Bismarck Tribune*; April 16, 2004):

> *FARGO — Republican congressional candidates Mike Liffrig and Duane Sand say Thursday's income tax filing deadline was painful, and they say the spending habits of Sen. Byron Dorgan and Rep. Earl Pomeroy should bear much of the blame.*
>
> *"It's an embarrassment because we're a moderate to conservative state," said Sand, who joined Liffrig on Thursday to promote a report by a watchdog group that lists the two Democrats among the biggest spenders in Congress...*

Note the date on the news story is April 16 – the press conference was held on *April 15* – tax day. If you have the right amount of creativity, a calendar – and a splash of timing – you'll do well in politics.

Frame the Issues ...

Ronald Reagan was a master at framing the issues. His ability to say unpleasant things in a pleasant manner made him a great communicator. Barry Goldwater, the conservative presidential candidate Reagan campaigned for in 1964 was the opposite. Senator Goldwater seemed to take pleasure in creating controversy. It's no surprise Ronald Reagan won election by a landslide while Barry Goldwater got 38 percent of the vote and won only 6 states.

If you want to be good at communications, it's important you learn to utilize the English language in a way that puts *you* in a favorable light. Different words have subtle inferences. For example, the word *philosophy* sounds positive while *ideology* sounds negative.

A biased liberal reporter will often describe a conservative as "the highly ideologically conservative Senator, Bob Smith." However, they will refer to "the philosophical Senator Hillary Clinton." They do this for a reason; they want to subtly influence public opinion. As a candidate, I recommend you pay close attention to the words you use.

Similarly, you would never say your candidate "reacted" to news. Instead you would say he, "responded" to it. (If you *react* to it, you've lost control of it. But if you *respond* to it, you've thought it out and acted in a methodical manner).

The point here is to make sure that you are using language in a way that accurately communicates your positive message.

Spin

According to Bill Press in *Spin This!*, "In its most innocent and innocuous form, spin is simply putting bad news in a better light. If you're dealt a handful of bad cards, bluff and pretend it's a royal flush. Or, as San Francisco's legendary advertising genius Jerry Mander once famously spun: 'When you're handed a lemon, make lemonade."

The expression derives from the spin given to a ball in sports like baseball and tennis in order to control the direction of the ball – or which way the ball bounces after impact.

Lesson Learned: Good and bad things happen on campaigns. It's up to you to present things that happen to you in a positive light.

Take a Stand and Be Optimistic

No matter how good you are at "spinning," you won't be a great communicator unless you also truly stand for something. One of the reasons Ronald Reagan was so popular was that he had a clear vision of what he wanted to do (namely restore hope and optimism in America and beat the Soviet Union). He was also optimistic. Before President Reagan came along, conservatives were anti-big government, anti-immigration, or anti-something. Reagan made conservatives pro-America and pro-family. From a marketing perspective, optimism sells. A corollary to that is that it's better to be *for* something than *against* something.

Have you ever noticed there are no groups calling themselves *Anti-Choice* or *Anti-Life*? These groups wisely labeled themselves Pro-Choice or Pro-Life. I've always thought that the National Right to Work Committee had a brilliant name. After all, they are *not* anti-union, they are pro-right to work!

Too many conservative candidates could give you a list of a hundred things they're against. But they'd be hard-pressed to give you a list of ten things that they're for. In 2000, Rick Lazio was criticized for this. He did a good job of telling voters why they shouldn't vote for Hillary Clinton. Unfortunately, he never gave the voters a good reason to vote for him. Don't get me wrong, candidates must present a case for why *not* to vote for their opponent. But as a candidate, you also must give the public a compelling reason to vote *for* you.

Our conservative message is positive. There is a lot more we're for than we are against. I'm for letting moms and dads keep more of what they earn, improving education, fixing transportation, and a strong national defense. Make sure that you aren't just talking about negative things. Start talking about all the positive things you are for.

Play the Expectations Game

During the 2000 campaign several important debates were held. It was important Bush do well. Yet anytime a Bush spokesman was asked about the upcoming debates, they'd always say: "Al Gore is one of the best debaters in the history of politics. If Governor Bush can just hold his own, we will consider it a victory."

The Bush campaign's method was counter-intuitive but brilliant. In essence, they said if Bush merely *survives* the debate, he will have "won." Likewise, if Al Gore doesn't mop the floor with him, Gore will have "lost." It worked. Bush gained momentum because of holding his own in the debates.

One of the most important tools in public relations is to *under-promise and over-achieve.* Set the bar of success low for yourself. Build your opponent up to a level he cannot achieve. This is counterintuitive to the self-promoter in you who wants to *hype* things.

During the 1992 Democrat Primary Election, Bill Clinton was able to convince the press that his second-place finish in the New Hampshire Primary actually proved his political resiliency (he had just come out of the Gennifer Flowers and draft controversies). By setting the bar low (at second place) he was able to "spin" the story to make it look as if he had won. That "victory" made Bill Clinton, "The Comeback Kid" (even though Paul Tsongas had beaten him by eight points).

Lesson Learned: Resist the urge to hype things. Always remember to under-promise, over achieve.

There's No Excuse for Not Having the Facts

Most of what's in this book is about the flashy and exciting aspects of politics (such as message and public speaking, etc.). But to be good at public relations, you can't just be a good talker, you must also understand the issues – and have a strong command of *the facts*.

There's no excuse for shoddy staff work. If you accuse your opponent of something, you'd better darn sure have the facts straight. If you are going to do an interview or a debate, you'd better have mastered the issues first.

Though "research" may seem boring, it is vital. Here's one example of how research paid off for me. On a congressional race, the local newspaper did a candidate profile on my candidate. They used a college professor to be the "unbiased expert" for the story. This professor was very negative regarding our campaign. Then, we discovered that this professor had actually donated to our opponent! Obviously, there was a conflict of interest. How can you be an "unbiased expert" if you have donated to one of the campaigns? Because we did the research, we were able to discredit the negative story, and get a "semi apology" from the newspaper.

The Forum (Fargo) published this "retraction" (sort of) story:

The Forum

by Mike Nawatzki
Published Wednesday, October 13, 2004

The campaign of North Dakota U.S. House challenger Duane Sand on Tuesday asked The Forum to admit using a "clearly biased source in an article previewing his race against incumbent Earl Pomeroy.

Mary Kweit, a political science professor and director of the Bureau of Governmental Affairs at the University of North Dakota in Grand Forks, was quoted in a preview of the Pomeroy-Sand race published in Sunday's edition of The Forum.

Campaign finance records show Kweit contributed $500 to Pomeroy's campaign on Nov. 24, 2003.

Sand's campaign manager, Matt Lewis, said Kweit and her husband, Robert Kweit -also a political science professor at UND - are known supporters of Democrats Pomeroy and North Dakota U.S. Sen. Byron Dorgan. Robert Kweit donated $500 to Dorgan on Dec. 26, 2002, campaign records show.

"The people who read this story in the paper on Sunday were misled," Lewis said. "They were led to believe they

were reading a nonpartisan critique of a campaign by a political science professional. But instead what they were getting is partisan rhetoric from a political hack."...

The Sand campaign also criticized The Forum for using Nick Barouth, an assistant political science professor at North Dakota State University, as another analyst in the article because he's only lived in the state since July.

Forum Editor Lou Ziegler said the reporter who wrote the story called the political science departments at both universities and asked to be referred to someone who could knowledgably speak about the race.

"He did not seek out any one individual," Ziegler said. "If we knew of Kweit's contribution, we wouldn't have interviewed her...

Lesson learned: Do the work. Do the research. It will pay huge dividends.

Chapter Two Lessons

The Basics
Your Crash-Course in Public Relations

- Being "right" on the issues isn't enough to win.
- Creativity is vital. But a creative idea at the wrong time *still* won't work.
- If you want to be good at communications, it's important you learn to utilize the English language in a way that puts you in a favorable light.
- Be positive. Give voters a reason to vote *for* you.
- Always under-promise and over-achieve
- Do the work. Do the research. There's no excuse for being sloppy.

CHAPTER THREE

The Vision Thing
It's the Message, Stupid!

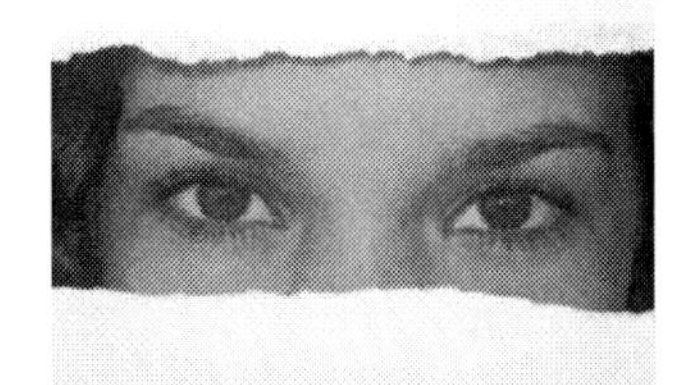

Photo taken by Marcos Santos

"Where there is no vision, the people perish."

-Proverbs 29:18

Developing your campaign's message is nothing more than packaging your vision into a message that folks will be able to easily understand and relate to. I know, it's easier said than done. That's why my friend, Mark Montini, developed a formula to help candidates develop their message. The *Montini Message Formula* says $M=EC^3$, or…**Message = Emotion x Contrast x Connection x Credibility.**

The Importance of Emotion

The first component your message must contain is emotion. Conservatives tend to be logical. We try to prove we're right through debate and intellectual discussion. We say things like, "The Rule of Law says this," or "The Constitution says that…"

Unfortunately, the vast majority of Americans don't think like us. They make their decisions based on emotion. If we want to win, we have to do a better job of conveying emotion.

Instead of saying, "The Founding Fathers never intended for us to pay these taxes," (a message that wouldn't resonate with the general public) talk about a family who has to scrape by just to put food on the table. And explain why it's the fault of the tax-and-spend liberals that this mom and dad can't afford to put Christmas presents under the tree this year.

Emotion Trumps Logic

I said earlier that there's no excuse for not having the facts. As a candidate or campaign manager, it's vital you understand policy and the issues. But the truth is that people make their decisions based on emotion, not on logic. I've heard it put this way: **Logic leads to conclusions, but emotion leads to action.**

Interestingly, I've always found that the most intelligent and philosophically motivated candidates are the ones who have the hardest time crafting an emotional message.

In his book, *Leadership*, Rudy Giuliani, recounts how he had to work with his media consultant, Roger Ailes, to help him overcome his training as an attorney. The following excerpt details a mock debate Mayor Giuliani had with Roger Ailes:

> *Playing the role of reporter, Roger said, "Mr. Giuliani, as a U.S. Attorney, you've had absolutely no involvement or responsibility of any kind for education. In fact, aside from going to school yourself, you don't know anything about education. Do you even have an educational plan? I replied, "Yes, I do, and let me tell you all about it. One, reform the board, two, do this, three, do that, four, do this…" I finished, and Roger started clapping. "Hey, great answer," he said. "I agree with all those things. You get an A for education – and an F for communication. "This isn't the United States Court of Appeals. Judges would remember those four points, and they'd write them down. But people at home aren't sitting there with a scorecard. Education – immediately, what does that say to you? Children. You have two minutes. The way you answer that question is, "I care greatly about children. I have my own. I've always loved children, and I care about*

them. And I realize that the future of our city is build around children. So the core of my concern about education is around children."

As Mayor Giuliani learned, politics isn't like high school debate class. The most logical and cogent argument doesn't always win. Instead, the argument that resonates with voters on an emotional level wins. Studies show that a logical argument leads people to conclusions. But emotion leads people to *action.*

Show the Contrast

In his book, *Flying Upside Down*, political consultant Joe Gaylord says, "A challenger must demonstrate three things in running against an incumbent: contrast, contrast, contrast." I've heard it put it this way: **In politics, unless you are *distinct*, you will become *extinct.***

To show contrast, you must be willing to stand for something. After the 2004 presidential campaign, some of John Kerry's own advisors lamented the fact that they had a hard time contrasting Kerry to Bush because Kerry's positions were constantly changing.

Unlike Kerry who tried to be "all things to all people," you must stress that there *are* big differences between you and your opponent. (The key, of course, is to stress the differences that favor you.) That's called "framing the debate."

When a candidate says, *"Let me tell you what this election is about,"* he is about to frame the debate. In short, he is going to talk about the differences between himself and the opponent that would show him in a favorable light (he will ignore the differences that would lead you to support his opponent). He knows that if this is the one contrast voters think about on Election Day, he will win.

Using contrast is just as important for local candidates to use as it is for presidential candidates. Suppose I'm a young guy running against a 16-year incumbent for state representative. My message would be, "If you want someone who is buddies with all the lobbyists in the state capital, then go ahead and vote for my opponent.

But if you want to vote for somebody who is going to bring change and represents *your* values, then vote for me."

On the other hand, if I'm the 16-year incumbent, I'm going to say, "If you want someone who is going to need training wheels and a map of the state capital, then vote for my opponent. But, if you want someone who's been fighting for you for 16 years, and who has brought home the bacon for this district, then why change horses in mid-stream? Vote for me."

Find Contrast Using The Leesburg Grid

In the early 1990s, several Republican leaders met in Leesburg, VA to discuss strategy. One of the most exciting things to come out of this meeting was *The Leesburg Grid.* In essence, it's a simple method for message development. Here's how it works:

Step 1: Draw a cross in the middle of a piece of paper.

Step 2: Assign the upper left quadrant for qualities you want the American people to attribute to you on Election Day. The upper right quadrant is what you want the American people to think about your opponent on Election Day. The lower left quadrant is designated for what your opponent wants people to think about him, and the lower right is what your opponent wants people to think about you. *Please note that, I'm using the 2000 Presidential race as an example. But you shouldn't assume that the Leesburg Grid is just for a high-level race. You ought to go through this exercise regardless of what race you're running for.*

Step 3: Draw a line connecting the "credible contrasts."

Note: The Leesburg Grid will not only help you craft your message, it will also help you predict where your opponent is going to attack you. Anything written in the lower right-hand quadrant is a weak spot for you. Make sure you are prepared to answer these attacks.

The Leesburg Grid

Bush vs. Gore (2000)

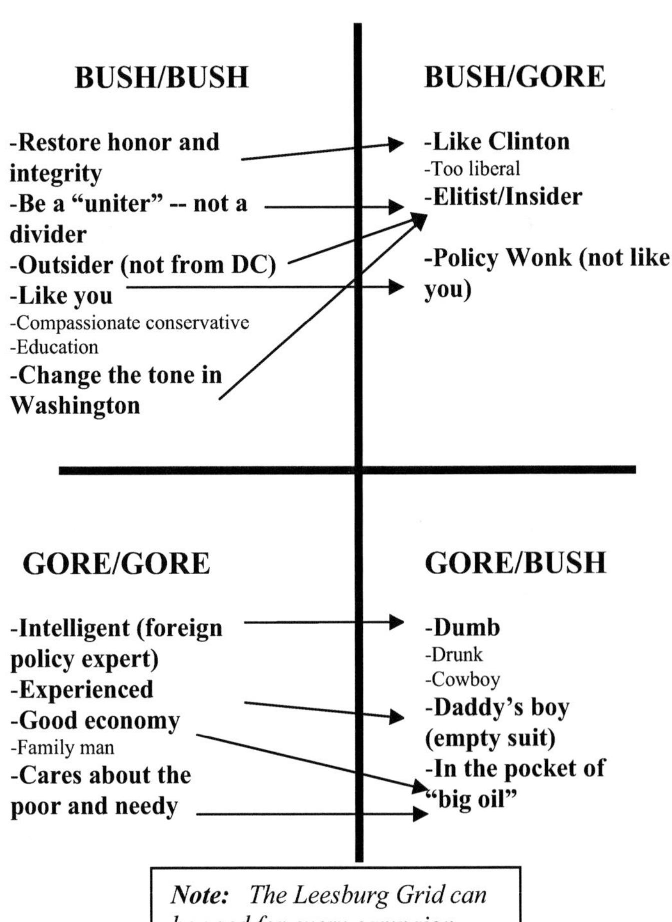

Note: The Leesburg Grid can be used for every campaign. I've used the 2000 Bush vs. Gore presidential race here because it is an example most readers would be familiar with.

Connect With the Voters

Every Republican candidate ought to add the following words to their vocabulary:

"Let me tell you what this means to you."

Many conservative candidates say things like, "I'm going to cut taxes by $1.6 billion over the next six fiscal years." (First of all, how many of us can fathom what $1.6 billion looks like? Have you ever seen a $1.6 billion bill?)

But not only are they using figures that few of us can relate to, they also fail to connect what a tax cut means to the individual they are talking to. They ought to say: *"I'm going to cut your taxes. Let me tell you what this means to you. This tax cut means you can pay for your daughters first 2 years of college when she turns 18."*

(The average person may not know what 1.6 billion dollars look like, but they can picture what 2 years of college will do for their daughter.)

Too many candidates say things like, "I'm going to fight crime." Instead, they should say: "I'm going to fight crime. Let me tell you what this means to you. It means you won't have to worry about your wife when she walks home from work in the evening."

Here's the point: When you're selling something to someone, always look at it from their perspective.

Many voters decide whom to vote for based on their immediate self interest. Don't assume voters will make the connection that a tax cut -- or even fighting crime -- is good for them.

You have to sell them the benefit. As they say in marketing, "sell the sizzle, not the steak." You literally have to say, "Now let me tell you what this means to you."

Without Credibility, Nothing Else Matters

In politics, your credibility is primarily derived from two things: character and competence.

As conservative icon, Morton Blackwell, says, "In politics, you have your word and your friends; go back on either and you're dead." That's because the most important part of the message formula is credibility. If you don't have a good reputation for honesty and a strong character, nothing else matters.

That's precisely why the first instinct of the Clinton War Room was to destroy the credibility of their detractors. Remember what James Carville said about Paula Jones? "Drag a $100 bill through a trailer park. You never know what you'll find." (Translation: It doesn't matter what she says because she's trash).

So how can your campaign gain – and keep – credibility? The first lesson to be learned is that you must always be honest. You won't be good at dealing with reporters if you don't have a relationship with them. And you can't have a good relationship with somebody that you lie to. If you ever get caught lying to a reporter, your credibility is toast.

Aside from character, your credibility also comes from your experience and competence.

Remember that what you're doing today will determine whether or not you're a credible candidate tomorrow. For example, if you plan to run for school board one day, you might want to start volunteering at a local school today. Your habits today (good or bad) will determine your credibility tomorrow.

Tell Your Story

Too many candidates want to run for office without "getting personal." In other words, they don't want to mention anything about their personal life, including their spouse or their children. The problem with that is that as a candidate, you're selling yourself. Your background is your credibility.

But for some reason, candidates think they're being "honorable" by leaving their family out of it and focusing on "the issues." In fact, they're being stupid. Truthfully, average people aren't going to vote for you because of the issues. They're going to vote for you because they like you.

Until 1988, when Michael Dukakis ran for president, he *refused* to talk about his heritage. In fact, he chose to lose elections rather than talk about it. This was a big mistake, given that his was a great story about a family achieving "the American dream." You see, both his parents emigrated from Greece, came to this country with very little, and became successful. It was a great story that a lot of people would have connected with…if they'd only known about it.

In 2000, I ran a school board race in Maryland. We ran a great campaign and ended up winning that race, even finishing ahead of the current president of the school board. Two days *after* the election, my candidate casually mentioned to me that both her brothers were school teachers.

During the campaign, my candidate was wrongly accused by her liberal opponents of all sorts of things, including being a "book burner." It would certainly have helped us to mention that, oh, by the way, both her brothers are teachers. But it never occurred to her that she should mention to me what her brothers did.

Another problem I've noticed is that a lot of candidates don't want to talk about their military experience. They somehow feel that it's not proper to do so. I wish I could shake them and get them out of that mindset. Military experience is an important part of who they are – and especially during this time in our nations' history – military experience is something that the voters are looking for in a leader.

The candidate can't be afraid to let the voters see who they are. They simply must be out there sharing their message and story, and casting their vision. They need to tell *their* story. Who are they? Where do they come from? Why are they running? How can I (as a voter) relate to them?

It's important to know their stance on the issues, but candidates need to explain who they are – the person – the one who stands out in the sleet and pumps gas; the person who waits in the checkout line at the grocery store – the person who sings in the church choir and coach's his son's little league team. As much as the candidate needs to cast the vision and stay on message, they need to be true to who they are and convey that fact to the public, as well. There are a lot of people who will vote for the person they feel they know and connect with. The bottom line is that the candidate *is* the message.

This is a Way of Life

Everything you do in a campaign should be done with $M=EC^3$ in mind. Whether you're writing a speech, designing your website, or preparing for a debate, ask yourself:

- "Is there emotion in this?"
- "How is this different from what everyone else is doing?"
- "Does this connect with regular people?"
- "Am I making a credible argument?"

- “Am I the right person to make this point?”

Use this as a guide for everything you do. Your speeches, your website, your door hangers…everything you do in a campaign.

Chapter Three Lessons

The Vision Thing
It's the Message, Stupid!

- Be emotional. Most voters make their decisions based on emotion…not logic.

- Elections are about choices. There must be contrast. You must find a way to show how your campaign is different than other campaigns.

- Connect with voters by saying: "Let me tell you what this means to you."

- Credibility is the most important part of your message. If people don't think you're a credible person, it doesn't matter what you say.

- If your message doesn't have emotion, contrast, connection, and credibility, it's not a good message.

- Don't be afraid to talk about your family and your personal life. Remember, you are the message.

CHAPTER FOUR

Repetition, Repetition, Repetition

The Beauty of staying "On Message"

"To control the campaign agenda, you need to get the media and your opponent talking about your issues."
-Joe Gaylord

The hardest thing in the world for most candidates to grasp is that it's the reporter's job to ask you tough questions, but it's your job to answer the questions you want to answer.

In his self-titled book, *Nofziger*, former Reagan Press Secretary, Lyn Nofziger, describes the importance of keeping your candidate "on message." "Most candidates have a compulsive urge to answer a question.

It was my job...to keep the candidate and the campaign on track. Otherwise, the other guy wins."

The good news is that once you've done the Leesburg Grid, it's much easier to stay "on message." Let me explain:

Referring back to the example of Bush vs. Gore, you can see that the credible contrasts that benefit Bush are:

1. Restoring honor and integrity to the office of the White House
2. The fact that he's a "uniter" – not a divider. And he will "change the tone" in Washington.
3. Likeability (he's more like you than Gore is).

In other words, if the most important thing a voter is thinking on Election Day is, "Which of these two guys is going to *restore integrity* to the White House…Bush wins.

However, referring back to the Leesburg grid, let's look at the issues that benefit Gore. They are as follows:

1. He's seen as being more intelligent.
2. Experience (Gore was a U.S. Senator and had been V.P. for eight years).
3. Cares about the poor and needy.

If a voter goes to the polls saying, "I want to vote for the candidate with the most *experience*,"

Gore wins. So, the key for Bush is to *stay on message* and make this election about the issues that favor him. In fact, I would submit to you that if Bush is talking about experience, he's losing. But if he's talking about integrity, he's winning.

In other words, if you look at the Leesburg Grid, Bush should never go below the centerline. To use a football analogy, the team that's on *offense* the longest usually wins most games. And if Bush is talking about experience, he's on defense.

In *The Art of War*, Sun Tzu says most battles are won before they're fought – and that the side that picks the terrain usually wins. The point is, according to the Leesburg Grid, Bush should spend his time talking about the issues that benefit him. Understanding this principle will greatly change the way you deal with reporters.

Examples

Here is a <u>*fictitious*</u> *example of a candidate that doesn't stay on message (based on the Leesburg Grid):*

Reporter: *"Governor Bush, most would agree that experience is important. Yet, you would have to agree that Vice President Gore has more experience than you..."*

Off-Message Bush: *"Well now you just wait a minute there. I was Governor of Texas, and my daddy was President..."*

Here's a fictitious example of staying on message.

Reporter: *"Governor Bush, most would agree that experience is important. Yet, you would have to agree that Vice President Gore has more experience than you..."*

On-Message Bush: *"The moms and dads that I talk to when I travel around America tell me the most important thing to them is electing a president who'll restore honor and integrity to the office of the White House..."*

Again, I've used the example of Bush vs. Gore, because it's an example that everyone can identify with. But don't think that this won't work for you, because it will.

If you're a young candidate running against an incumbent, and they ask you about experience, you can say, *"The moms and dads that I talk to when I am campaigning throughout our district tell me the most important thing to them is electing someone who will bring change and new energy to the office."*

Conversely, the incumbent might answer, *"The moms and dads that I talk to when I go door-to-door campaigning, tell me the most important thing to them is having someone with the leadership experience to go to the State Capital and fight for them. They tell me they can't afford to trust the business of government to someone who still needs training wheels."*

How the Clinton Team Used This Technique

In their book, *Buck Up, Suck Up...And Come Back When You Foul Up*, James Carville and Paul Begala recount an interview Paul Begala did on *Meet the Press.* According to the book:

> *"At least a dozen times in that interview, Russert asked Paul why Clinton wouldn't simply tell the American people the true nature of his relationship with Monica Lewinsky. And at least as many times Paul responded by decrying the tactics of the Starr operation. Afterward, the interview made a front-page, above-the-fold story in The New York Times. Tim later told Paul, 'We both did our jobs.'"*

Why did Paul keep bringing up Ken Starr? Because if he's talking about Monica, he's losing. But if he's talking about Ken Starr, he's winning.

Candidates tend to believe that reporters will personally resent them for staying "on message." But note that Tim Russert didn't mind the fact that Begala was "staying on message." In fact, Tim congratulated him on doing his job.

In *Media Smart, How to Handle a Reporter, By a Reporter*, author Dennis Stauffer dismisses the idea that reporters resent candidates who stay on message: "(Candidates) may use the same key sentence in interviews with several different reporters...Rather than object to such practices, reporters tend to criticize the official who isn't 'savvy enough' to give us something we can use."

Repetition, Repetition, Repetition...

Too many candidates are really smart people who get bored easily. For this reason, they resent being told to stay on message. The truth is being repetitious will result in your being remembered. (The caveat is that you must have a message that "sells." Repeating a bad message will certainly not help you.) It doesn't do you any good to come up with a really good message that utilizes emotion, contrast, connection, and credibility – unless you're willing to repeat your talking points over and over again.

"Talking Points" says Bill Press in his book *Spin This!* "are a list of points a politician should make when asked a question about a given topic...No matter what the question, the politician should make those points and only those points."

How many times do you think Bush said he was going to be "a uniter not a divider" during the 2000 election? How many times do you think Bush said he was going to "restore honor and integrity?" Why did he repeat it so many times? Because that's what it took to get his message out. You see, studies show the average person has to hear something seven times before they begin to remember it. But how many times does someone have to say something before the average person actually hears it seven times? No doubt hundreds – or thousands of times.

Remember Bill Clinton's 1992 campaign message?

Change vs. More of the Same
The economy, stupid
Don't forget health care

As George Stephanopoulos recounts in his book, *All Too Human*: "I thought of it as a campaign haiku – an entire election manifesto condensed to nineteen syllables. James (Carville) drilled it into our heads, and every speech, every event, every attack, and every response had to reflect one of these three statements…"

Before you start being repetitious, I must warn you of a couple of things:

- *Repetition will annoy your spouse and your closest supporters*. Your friends and family are at *every* debate. They read *every* article. They listen to *every* radio ad. So, it's no surprise *they* think everyone is sick of hearing the same old lines. **We use repetition because the average person spends only about seven minutes per week thinking about politics.**

- *Repeating a good message will draw the ire of your opponents.* Once you find a good message that resonates with voters, your opponent will attack you for using it. (Most likely, they will say you are "going negative".) Rest assured, the reason they're attacking you is because it's working.

Taking the negatives into account, it's vital your campaign utilizes repetition. As Theodore Roosevelt once said, "If you want any new notions and impressions to sink in and spread across a continent, you have to iterate and reiterate and emphasize and drive home, until you are pretty well weary of the very sound of your own voice."

If that sentiment was true in the time of Theodore Roosevelt, it's certainly true today. In our media culture, you and I are constantly barraged with messages. Every day, each of us probably listens to the radio, watches TV, surfs the internet, talks on the phone, and drives past countless billboards – each of which is trying to "sell" us something.

In order to survive, we've had to learn to "tune-out" these messages. In short, we've become desensitized. That's precisely why (if you want your message to sink in) you have to repeat it over and over again.

Chapter Four Lessons

Repetition, Repetition, Repetition

The Beauty of Staying "On Message"

- Remember that it's a reporter's job to ask you tough questions, but it's *your* job to answer the questions you want to answer.

- Talk about the issues that benefit you. Time is a scarce commodity. Use your time to talk about the issues that you want to talk about.

- Interestingly, reporters will respect you more if you stay "on message."

- You've got to repeat your message a zillion times, plus one.

- Once you've got a good message, your opponent will attack you for using it. Don't let this deter you. Stay the course. They wouldn't attack you unless your message was working!

CHAPTER FIVE

What Most Americans Really Fear

Public Speaking Made Easy

"Of all the talents bestowed upon men, none is so precious as the gift of oratory...Abandoned by party, betrayed by his friends, stripped of his offices, whoever can command this power is still formidable."

-Winston Churchill

Few skills can help a candidate as much as the ability to speak well in public. The good news is that each of us can learn to become better at public speaking.

This chapter comes after the chapter on developing your message for a reason. Even the most eloquent speech will be judged a failure if it doesn't convey the campaign's message. The most important question you must ask yourself before giving a speech is, *"What is my goal?"*

The great Athenian orator, Demosthenes, was asked what three things made for a great speech. His answer was, "action, action, action."

Each speech you give must be for a reason, because at some point, you must challenge the audience to take action. If the primary goal of this particular speech is to inspire people to vote, then you'd give one type of speech. If your primary goal is to make sure everyone knows how evil your opponent is – use a different kind of speech. But before giving a speech, make sure you know what your goal is.

Again, it doesn't matter how eloquent a speaker you are, if you're not communicating – and repeating your message – you probably won't win your election.

Once you've decided what your goal is, here are some tips for how to deliver it more effectively:

Practice Like You Play

The key to improve your speaking is to practice like you play. In other words, if you want to stop using fillers, such as umm, when you are speaking in pubic -- you've got to eliminate them from your everyday life, too.

If you want to quit pointing at your audience during a speech, you've got to quit pointing during your everyday conversations. If you want to start using inclusive language during your speeches, you've got to make it part of your life. You can't wait until you're on stage to change things. When you're under pressure and nervous, you will revert to the habits you've developed over time.

My dad was a correctional officer for over twenty years. He told me this story:

Every year, correctional officers have to qualify on the same firing range as regular police officers. In the old days, this was considered a "day off." Officers would show up in blue jeans and they got in the bad habit of keeping their ammunition in their back pocket. The problem with that is that they don't wear blue jeans to work.

One day a police officer was involved in a shoot out with a drug dealer. He ran out of ammunition, and was found dead with his hand in his back pocket (looking for ammunition that wasn't kept there). Under pressure, this police officer reverted to his training. Unfortunately, his training had prepared him to look for bullets in the wrong place.

My point is that if you want to be good on stage, you've got to develop good habits off stage. Because when the pressure is on, you will revert to what you've practiced. You've got to become "unconsciously-competent."

What you do daily will become second nature to you. As I once heard a preacher say, "Men don't determine their future. They determine their habits, and their habits determine their future."

Lesson Learned: To be a good speaker you must develop and practice good habits before you get behind a podium.

How You Look

Let's face it. People judge us (rightly or wrongly) based on how we look. I'm not necessarily talking about how physically attractive we are. I'm talking about a more elusive quality. It has less to do with attractiveness than it does with seriousness and likeability. Likeability is a vital factor in politics.

During a November 4, 2003 episode of *Hardball with Chris Matthews*, Rep. Dick Gephardt described why people like Bush: "I think he is a nice guy…I think people like him. You know, the old story is they'd like to go have a beer with him."

Unfortunately, too many Republican candidates don't understand just how important appearance is in politics. The following pie chart is based on a famous study conducted in the 1970s. It demonstrates just how important appearances are in politics:

How an Audience Judges You

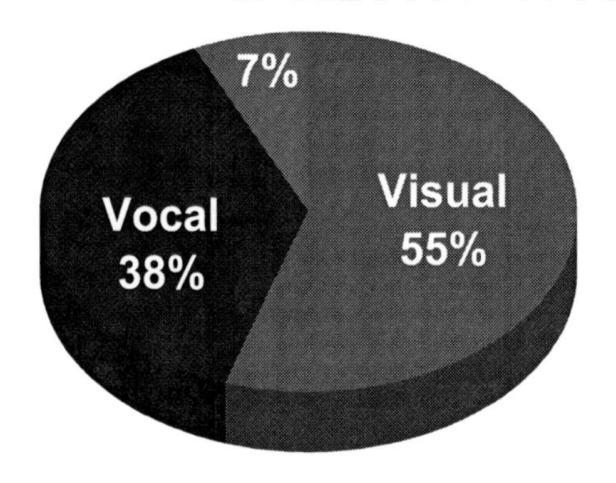

As you can see, 55 percent of the way an audience judges you is based on visuals. The quality of your voice accounts for 38 percent. <u>And here's the kicker: *the actual words you use account for only 7 percent of how an audience judges you*.</u>

Most candidates spend 100 percent of their time trying to *write* "the perfect speech." They worry about crafting just the right words. They'll stay up until 3 am laboring over the second word in the sixth paragraph of a policy paper. *They spend 100 percent of their time focusing on what yields them just 7 percent of the results.*

Few candidates spend the same amount of time picking out their wardrobe, video taping their speeches, or working with a voice coach. They spend zero percent of their time working on the things that really matter to their audience.

In *The Power Game*, author Hendrick Smith quotes former Democrat presidential candidate Paul Tsongas on the importance of visuals verses content.

"People would come up to me and say, 'I saw you on television last week,' and I'd say, 'Oh, what was it about?' and they'd say, 'Well I don't remember, but you looked tired,' or 'I liked your tie.'"

Smith also quotes Nixon regarding his 1960 loss to Jack Kennedy: "I spent too much time…on substance and too little time on appearance. I paid too much attention to what I was going to say and too little to how I would look." (As you'll recall, people who heard the 1960 debate on the radio said Nixon won. But people who watched the debate on television said Kennedy won.)

Lesson Learned: To be a good communicator, pay attention to how you look. Video tape yourself and study how to come across in a positive manner.

Body Language

Considering that the primary way an audience judges you is visually, body language is very important because an audience is more likely to judge you by what your body tells them than by the words you speak.

Based on your body language, an audience can sense whether or not you're confident. And if you're not, then your credibility goes out the window.

In her book, *The Polished Politician*, political image consultant, Lillian Brown, offers advice for candidates who struggle with confidence:

> *Walk, talk, dress and think like a successful candidate who has been elected and is already in office. As you run for public office, be it a local school board election or a U.S. Senate seat, visualize yourself occupying the office which you aspire. Voters want to trust you and feel they are making the right choice.*

In addition to exuding confidence, you must also work to use inclusive body language. For example, the best communicators never point. Pointing implies you are *lecturing* or that you are a "mean" conservative.

I took this picture at a Howard Dean rally in Fargo, ND. As you can see, pointing sends a negative message.

Practice using open-handed gestures. In eight years of his presidency, I can only recall Bill Clinton pointing once. It was when he said "I did not have sexual relations with that woman…"

Videotape yourself speaking and see how you come across. Do you look friendly on tape? For example, during question and answer sessions, leaning forward signifies you are interested in the other person, while folding your arms tells the other person that you're not listening – or that you disagree with them.

Phyllis Schlafly of the conservative organization Eagle Forum has a great way of illustrating this point. She says you can tell who's winning a debate by simply turning the volume down on the television and watching the body language.

When speaking in public, you must communicate that you are confident and passionate about what you're saying.

As famed motivational author, Dale Carnegie, said: "This is the day of dramatization. Merely stating a truth isn't enough. The truth has to be made vivid, interesting, dramatic. You have to use showmanship. The movies do it. Television does it. And you will have to do it if you want attention."

Eye Contact

They say "the eyes are the windows to the soul," and most audiences would agree with that assessment. People who give direct eye contact are viewed as strong and trustworthy. People who refuse to make eye contact are thought to be hiding something.

Many public speaking classes wrongly advise students to "look over the heads of the audience." After all, they say, "the audience will believe you are looking at them."

I believe this to be one of the worst pieces of advice a speaker could receive. First of all, most candidates aren't running for president. They're likely to spend most of their time speaking to audiences consisting of fifty or so people. In that environment you must make eye contact throughout your speech with nearly everyone

in the audience (making sure that you cover every area of the room). (Obviously, if you're reading your speech, this will be difficult. But since you're not going to be reading to your audience, it'll be much easier to do than you think.)

Even if you're speaking to a large group of hundreds of people, you should still pick out various people in the audience to make eye contact with. But be assured: Merely looking over the heads of the audience will not fool anyone. It'll just make you look weird.

Don't Read to Your Audience

It's impossible to read to your audience and make good eye contact. Candidates read their speeches because they're more concerned about saying just the right thing than they are about how they look or come across to the audience.

According to Jennifer Hoff, a public relations specialist for legislators in the Michigan House of Representatives, "If you focus on reading the words of the speech, rather than reaching out to the audience with eye contact, you could leave the impression that the message or words are more important than the people affected by them."

Don't get me wrong, if you're delivering something as important as the State of the Union address, you'd certainly use the TelePrompTer. But that's the exception. The points you'll score for being a good speaker will outweigh the fact that you might have missed a point or two that you meant to make. If you must rely on notes, that's fine. Use 3 x 5 cards. Just remember, the primary way an audience judges you is visually.

The Importance of a Smile

Smiling is an important part of being a good communicator – especially for conservatives who've long been stereotyped as "mean." Obviously, there are subjects in which you wouldn't want to smile. However, the vast majority of the time you're on television – or simply giving a speech – you ought to smile.

Look at how positive J.C. Watts always looks on television. I can guarantee you that the primary reason people view him favorably is because of his contagious smile.

Smiling isn't easy, especially when you're nervous. The truth is that sometimes you'll have to *make* yourself do it. It'll feel really cheesy at first. But trust me, to be a good communicator in today's political world it's probably the single most vital thing you have to make yourself do. In addition, you'll find that smiling affects a lot of things, such as vocal quality. That's why telemarketing companies put mirrors at the workstations of their employees.

Dress for Success

A while ago, I saw a Leonardo DiCaprio movie called *Catch Me If You Can*. The movie was based on the true story of a con artist who was able to fool people into believing he was an airline pilot and a surgeon. In the movie, once people saw DiCaprio dressed in a pilot's uniform they automatically trusted him. I think most of us are the same way. The way someone dresses – as well as their body language – sends a signal to us about how we should think of them.

Think this is only a modern phenomenon that is a result of today's superficial society? Think again. In his book, *Speak Like Churchill, Stand Like Lincoln*, James C. Humes recounts the great efforts George Washington took to look like a leader:

> *As Reagan did centuries later, (George) Washington viewed the presidency as theater. He made it a traveling show by taking a carriage to cities and towns of the new states. Just outside the city, he would get out of the carriage, brush off his clothes, and buff his boots. Then he would mount Prescott, his white stallion, to stage his procession into the city.*

You may not be running for president, but your appearance is important if you want to be successful as a politician at any level.

The key to looking good is to dress one step above the best-dressed person in your audience. If you're at a 4th of July picnic and the best dressed person there is wearing a tee shirt and shorts, you should wear a polo and khaki pants. If you're at a meeting where the best-dressed person is wearing a polo and khaki's, you ought to wear a blazer.

Err on the side of dressing conservatively. For men, having a good blue suit and shined black shoes goes a long way. Campaign staff should always pack an extra blazer, shirt, and necktie for the candidate (wherever he goes). That way, if something spills, you just change jackets. For ladies, again, the key is to dress conservatively. Avoid earrings that are bigger than a dime, and avoid wearing pins and brooches.

Be a Good Story Teller

Be it Reagan, Lincoln, or Churchill, the best speakers are also good story tellers. Jesus spoke in parables for a reason: Stories connect with regular folks. If you're serious about politics, I highly recommend you begin building a repertoire of good stories you can tell. There is one caveat, however; the stories must be true. In his 2000 presidential campaign, Al Gore used stories to illustrate his points. However, he ran into problems because the stories he told simply were not true.

Challenge: Start memorizing good stories to tell.

Use Inclusive Language

One of the first lessons to learn in public speaking is to use *inclusive language*. Remember when Ross Perot addressed the NAACP and referred to the audience as, "*you people*?" He broke a cardinal rule of public speaking – be inclusive! The good speakers won't make *that* mistake. Listen to a Reagan speech and count the number of times he says the words, "*you and I*." Take a lesson from "The Gipper" and make sure your speeches and press releases use inclusive language. And remember: "You and I have a rendezvous with destiny."

Know When to Shut Up

You'll never hear a complaint that your speech was too brief. Lincoln's Gettysburg Address is a prime example. The speaker who preceded Lincoln was Edward Everett, a famed orator of the time. On that day, Everett spoke for more than two hours. His long-winded speech has been forgotten, but Lincoln's 272-word speech is considered one of the greatest speeches ever written.

Winston Churchill once gave an entire speech where all he said was: "Never, never, never, never, never give in – except to dictates of honor and good sense." As a candidate, you'll do well to copy Lincoln and Churchill, and keep it brief.

Knowing when to shut up is a skill that few candidates have. It's always better to "end on top." If you're nearing the end of your speech and you get a standing ovation, just end it there. Act as if your speech is over. You're not likely to do better than a standing ovation.

Comedian Jerry Seinfeld understood the importance of getting out on top. By ending his television show *Seinfeld* while it was still on top in the ratings, he went out on his own terms. That's smart politics, too.

Your *Real* Audience

A lot of state and local candidates attempt to attend *every* debate or "candidate forum" they're invited to. Obviously, you should try to attend important debates. But often these sparsely attended candidate forums occur every night of the week.

Frankly, my experience is that these candidates would reach more undecided voters if they randomly called people in the phone book. That's because the average undecided voter rarely goes to these forums. Many candidates end up spending their valuable time with a moderator – and a crowd that consists of their opponents – and their opponent's families.

In this type of situation, it's important for a candidate to understand who the *real* audience is. Your *primary audience* is the people in front of you. That might include the moderator, your opponents, and the people in the crowd (all of whom have probably already made up their minds for whom to vote).

But your *real* audience is the important audience. Your real audience isn't the fifty people in the crowd. It's the 100,000 people who will read your quotes in the newspaper the next day.

In 1992, Ross Perot addressed the Christian Coalition. Realistically, he must have known that most of the thousand or so people in the audience weren't going to vote for *him*. So why did he address the audience? Because he knew that the crowd would be respectful to him – and that his real audience (millions of rank-and-file Christians who might vote for him) would see him on television.

Lesson Learned: Keep in mind your real audience might not be the people in the room with you.

Pause (Instead of Saying "Umm")

If you want to be a great speaker, you'll have to avoid using fillers such as, "umm." These fillers are annoying, and worse, make you sound unconfident. People use fillers out of habit. They developed this habit because they are afraid of silence.

When someone asks you a question, waiting ten seconds might seem like an eternity to you, but it's not. There's nothing wrong with silence – in fact, it can have a disarming affect. As Charles deGaule said, "Silence is the ultimate weapon of power."

In his book, *Speak Like Churchill, Stand Like Lincoln*, author James C. Humes notes that many of the best political leaders have utilized this "Power Pause" technique. According to Humes, "Napoleon is among the most dominant of personalities in the world history because, among other factors, he knew the keys to charisma. The Power Pause method was his key to magnifying his message."

Chapter Five Lessons

What Most Americans Really Fear
Public Speaking Made Easy

- The most important question you must ask yourself before speaking is, "What is my goal?"
- A good speech asks the audience to take action.
- The primary way an audience judges you is visually. The words you speak only account for 7 percent of the way an audience judges you.
- The best speakers are good story tellers. Work on building a file of good stories to tell.
- You'll never hear a complaint that your speech was *too* brief.
- Ascertain who your "real audience" is. Hint: it may not be the people in the room with you.

CHAPTER SIX

Pushing Your Campaign
Getting Your Story to the Media

"Without promotion, something terrible happens, NOTHING!"
-P.T. Barnum

In the movie *Jerry McGuire*, there's a flash-back scene where Jerry remembers the words of his late mentor, Dicky Fox, who says: "The key to this business is personal relationships." That advice should also be headed by campaigns, because the key to this business *is* personal relationships.

Spend a lot of time developing a good rapport with reporters. Take them out to lunch. Let them see you're a decent person. Even if the reporter is a liberal, it's going to be hard for them to think you're "an evil conservative" after you've just had a grilled cheese and tomato soup with them.

Understanding Reporters

It's important for you to know what a reporters "bottom line" is. Each reporter is different. Some are looking for a controversial story that will make them the next Woodward or Bernstein. Some are biased, but persuadable. Some like content, while others like "process" (the horserace aspect of a campaign). It's your job to "get inside their heads" and figure out what makes them tick.

It's safe to assume the most important thing to a reporter is keeping his or her job. That means ultimately that their story must be exciting enough to help sell newspapers. If you can give them an exciting story, they might publish it. But make no mistake, reporters don't need you…you *need* them.

Your job is to find a way to get your message out. If one newspaper in your town is biased against you, you may have to work hard to get the weekly papers, the A.P. Reporter, or the local talk show host on your side. This may take an incredible amount of charm and effort. Invite them to lunch. Get to know them. Build relationship. The odds are they are competing with the newspaper that doesn't like you – and may not like that newspaper any more than you do.

The Most Important Question

The most important question you will likely ever be asked in an interview is, *"Why are you running?"* In

1980, Ted Kennedy couldn't come up with an answer to that question, and it ended his presidential campaign. Likewise, if you don't have a good answer to this basic question, that doesn't include your lusting for power, then you'd better go back to the drawing board.

Even the best public relations expert would have a hard time "selling" a candidate who doesn't have a vision. Take time to make sure you know exactly what it is that you believe in – and why you are running.

Socrates said, "The unexamined life is not worth living." The Matt Lewis version is: "The unexamined campaign is not worth running."

Some candidates are good speakers, but have no convictions. Other candidates have deep convictions, but cannot communicate them effectively. Ronald Reagan was the perfect marriage of philosophy and campaign smarts; he had deeply held convictions – *and* he knew how to communicate them.

Never Lie

Spinning (presenting your campaign in the best possible light) is acceptable. Lying is not. To some, it may be hard to see where the line is. *In Spin This!,* Bill Press puts it this way: "For practitioners, there's one difference: If you're caught spinning once, no problem. You can spin again and again. If you're caught lying once, you're dead."

In 2001, football coach, George O'Leary, was forced to resign his newly appointed position of head football coach at Notre Dame University. O'Leary's résumé had exaggerated his level of education (he has a bachelor's degree, not a master's) and exaggerated his college football accomplishments. The unfortunate part is that his lack of a master's degree probably wouldn't have kept him from getting the job at Notre Dame. After all, he had good experience and obviously understands the game of football. But the fact that he lied about his past couldn't be overlooked. Let this be a lesson to each of us. If exaggerating a resume can force a great football coach like George O'Leary to resign, what do you think it'll do to you as a candidate?

Don't Get Mad...Get Ahead

There will no doubt be times when you disagree with what is written about you. An old saying in politics is, "Don't pick a fight with someone who buys ink by the barrel and paper by the ton." No matter how badly a reporter treats you, you won't get ahead by yelling at a reporter.

On the other hand, many reporters follow the path of least resistance. If you're running against an incumbent, a wimpy reporter might think twice about writing a negative story if he knows the incumbent is going to give him a hard time about it. If your opponent complains – but you never do – then you're likely to get more bad press.

In a 1992 interview with the *Washington Post*, RNC Chairman Rich Bond used a baseball analogy to illustrate this point:

"If you watch any great coach, what they try to do is work the refs. Maybe the ref will cut you a little slack next time."

I remember hearing a story about a baseball player who grew up being told that you should never argue with an umpire on balls and strikes. His philosophy was to just do the best he could, and that umpires would respect him for never disagreeing with them. He later learned that this theory was wrong. He started observing that the players who make their disapproval known to the umpire get better calls in the future.

Lesson Learned: If a reporter writes a bad story about you, call him and give your side. Who knows, maybe next time, he will try to err on your side to make up for it. But remember: never get mad – except on purpose.

Pitching the Story

As conservative icon Morton Blackwell says, "Nothing moves in politics unless it's pushed." Sometimes you will have to call a reporter on the phone and sell them on covering a story – or at least covering it the way you see it. There is a subtle difference between being aggressive and being annoying. You must be aggressive, but never cross the line (easier said than done).

Part of being good at selling your story is getting to know each reporter as an individual. I must confess that you will have to play psychologist and try to get inside the head of each reporter you're dealing with (don't worry, they are also doing this to you).

Ask yourself, what does this particular reporter want in a story? Some reporters are really gossip columnists at heart. They like the juicy stuff. Other reporters like "process." They are more likely to do a story on a poll that just came out than they are to cover an issue briefing. Knowing what your reporter is like will tell you who to approach with a particular story – and how to sell it to them.

Never discount the personal relationship. Some reporters I've dealt with I approach like a poker buddy. For other reporters, I may have an innocent flirty relationship with them (these are female reporters). Either way, it's up to you to know what makes them tick.

Media Releases

Once you've developed a working relationship with a reporter, one of the ways to tell *your* story is to send out a media release. Collect a list of all the media outlets in your area and the names of the reporters who cover the political beat for them.

Your media list should contain their contact info, as well as the time of their deadline. Most importantly, you should denote how *they'd* like to receive info. Do they prefer fax, email, or hand-delivery of press releases?

Since you need the media more than they need you, it's your job to cater to them. Also, before sending a media release, consider whether or not this is really news.

Remember the boy who cried: "Wolf"? If you fax pointless media releases every day, the media will start ignoring your releases. Make sure it's really news.

Don't Sound Opinionated

When you write a media release you want to write it as if you were writing a news story. That means you don't want it to *sound* opinionated. The reason for this is that, occasionally, reporters (particularly for smaller, weekly papers) will publish your press release verbatim (if it sounds like real news).

But your job isn't to be a reporter; it's to get *your* message out. So, how do you write a press release that sounds un-opinionated but actually gets your campaign's message out? **The way to do it is to use quotes that favor you.**

Following is an example of a media release I wrote:

NFIB ENDORSES DUANE SAND

June 30, 2004 Contact: Matt Lewis (701) 237-6700

FARGO: America's largest advocacy organization representing small and independent businesses has endorsed Duane Sand for Congress.

According to a letter from the National Federation of Independent Business' (NFIB) political action committee, SAFE (*Save America's Free Enterprise*): "Men and women around the country are living the American dream of owning their own business and they need your (Duane Sand's) support in Congress to protect a pro-free-enterprise environment for their success."

"I'm honored to receive the endorsement of America's largest pro-small business organization," said Sand.

According to Sand campaign manager Matt Lewis: "Duane Sand knows what it's like to risk his life's savings to invest in small businesses in rural America. As such, Duane will fight to keep the Bush tax cuts which have been a God-send for farmers and small businesses in

North Dakota. The bottom line is that Duane has personally created jobs. Earl Pomeroy hasn't."

As you can see, the most important points about my candidate appeared in the *quotes*. We used the quotes to stress his background as a small business owner and to contrast him with our opponent. Here's how *The National Journal's Hotline* (www.NationalJournal.com) covered this media release:

NORTH DAKOTA AT-LARGE SAFE?

America's "largest" advocacy organization representing small and indep. businesses has endorsed '00 nominee/ex-Navy officer **Duane Sand** (R).

According to a letter from the NFIB's PAC -- SAFE (Save America's Free Enterprise): "Men and women around the country are living the American dream of owning their own business and they need your (Duane Sand's) support in Congress to protect a pro-free-enterprise environment for their success." According to

Sand Campaign Manager **Matt Lewis**: "Duane Sand knows what it's like to risk his life's savings to invest in small businesses in rural America. As such, Duane will fight to keep the **Bush** tax cuts which have been a God-send for farmers and small businesses in North Dakota. The bottom line is that Duane has personally created jobs. **Earl Pomeroy** hasn't" (Sand release, 6/30).

Media releases should be written in the "inverse triangle" format. That means that you include the most important information (for your campaign) in the beginning, and the least important at the end. The reason for this is that (in order to save space) reporters will sometimes chop off the end of your story before printing it. If you've waited until the end of the story to get your message out, your message will end up on the cutting-room floor.

This media release was good because:

- The media basically re-printed the press release.
- It was controversial enough to pique the interest of a reporter.
- The headline catches your attention.
- Our quotes portrayed our side of the story.

"Off-The-Record" Doesn't Exist

Earlier I talked about how important it is to develop a personal relationship with a reporter. This is not to be confused with becoming "friends" with a reporter. In his excellent book, *Hardball,* Chris Matthews recounts how someone becomes a reporter. To paraphrase, after journalism school, the first job you get as a reporter is to investigate gruesome deaths like car accidents. As a new reporter, you get the unpleasant job of interviewing the widow, etc. Nine out of ten people can't stomach that job. The ones who excel at it become political reporters.

Although I highly recommend developing a good rapport with reporters, I want to stress that they are not your friends. You've probably heard of the terms, "off-the-record," "on-the-record," "background," and "deep background." The truth is – as far as you're concerned – everything you say to a reporter is "on-the-record." There are no laws governing these "rules" of journalism. **Always assume any thing you say could end up on the front page of the Washington Post.**

Never Take a Reporter's Call...

A candidate should *never* accept a reporters' "cold" call. During a campaign, all sorts of accusations are made. And no matter how skilled you are, unless you are prepared...you will eventually say something stupid.

Before talking to a reporter about any subject, the candidate should have talking points. He should have done the Leesburg grid, and considered how the talking points can utilize $M=EC^3$. And the candidate should talk to his consultant *before* doing the interview.

Following is an example of how a reporter's call should be handled:

REPORTER: "Hi. Is Matt there?"

COMMUNICATIONS DIRECTOR: "I'm sorry, the candidate is right in the middle of something. Can I help you?

REPORTER: "Look, this is John with the Fredericktown Post. I must talk to Matt right now because my deadline is in five minutes.

COMMUNICATIONS DIRECTOR: "I'm sorry. Matt is in the middle of meeting with someone. I promise to have him call you back in exactly five minutes. What can I tell him this is in regards to?

REPORTER: "Okay. I'm in a big hurry. Basically, it's in regards to the yard signs which your opponent claims you tore down."

Now you at least have time to come up with some talking points to give the reporter.

Make sure to explain this to your volunteers and staff at the headquarters. They should *never* transfer a media cold-call to the candidate. Instead, train them to transfer the call to the communications director or take a detailed message. Also, make sure they are instructed not to give the candidate's cell phone number to ANYBODY…especially the media!

"Iffy" Questions

"If I've learned one thing in my nine days in politics, it's you better be careful with hypothetical questions," declared Gen. Wesley Clark in a 2003 presidential candidates' debate. Harry Truman put it this way: "I don't answer iffy questions."

As a candidate, you should never answer hypothetical questions. If a reporter asks you, "What would you do if…" or "If such and such were to happen, would you…" don't fall for it. They're laying a trap for you. Nothing good can come from answering that sort of question.

In an effort to avoid hypothetical questions (or any questions) make sure *not* to say: "No comment." In today's world saying, "No comment" is code for, "I'm guilty." Instead, simply say: "I'm not interested in talking hypothetically.

In addition to answering hypothetical questions, candidates should not feel compelled to answer questions that weren't asked. The candidate should only answer questions they are asked. Too many times a candidate feels the need to explain their position on the issue. There is a time and a place for that. When dealing with the media, however, a candidate should only answer the question presented to them. If the media want to know why you are pro-life, let them ask it.

Use Technology

Great politicians always take advantage of new technology. FDR mastered radio; Kennedy and Reagan mastered television. More recently, John McCain and Howard Dean have done a good job of utilizing the internet.

Today, every campaign should be utilizing technology to deliver their message. If your candidate gives a speech, you ought to be able to record it digitally. It's inexpensive to purchase the Olympus DM series digital tape recorder (I recommend using Windows Media format) to edit and email the quotes you'd like to hear on the radio – or see in print – to the media.

A radio station may not have the resources to send a reporter to cover your press conference. But if you have a good relationship with a reporter, you might get a good quote to run on the local news if you email them a digital recording. Likewise, take digital pictures and email them to the print media.

Every campaign manager should have instant messenger. It's great for instant communication with consultants. Just go to www.aim.org and download Aol's instant messenger for free.

In his book *Power Plays*, Dick Morris says that using a new technology can be: "…Like the first warriors who met bows and arrows with gunfire – or like America in 1945, using the atomic bomb to bring an end to the war with Japan…"

Using technology also sends a subtler message: If *you're* using it – and your opponent isn't – it implies that your campaign is more progressive than your opponent. As Joe Gaylord says, "If you don't ensure that your campaign is in the Information Age, it may as well be in the Dark Ages."

Chapter Six Lessons

Pushing Your Campaign
Getting Your Story to the Media

- Spend a lot of time and energy developing a good rapport with reporters. (This is not to be confused with becoming "friends" with a reporter.)
- Before sending a press release, make sure it's really news.
- When you write a media release, write it as if you were writing a *news story.*
- Assume anything you say to a reporter could end up on the front page of a newspaper.
- Avoid answering hypothetical questions.

CHAPTER SEVEN

Coffee and Donuts Go a Long Way

Media Releases and News Events

"We had a rule in the Nixon operation, that before any public event was put on his schedule, you had to know what the headline out of that event was going to be, what the picture was going to be, and what the lead paragraph would be."

-David Gergen

The first thing to think about when considering holding a news conference is: Do I really need to have this event? Candidate's frequently mistake action for accomplishment. They like how it looks to have a big crowd gathered to hear them speak. Their ego wants them to have events, but there may be no strategic advantage for doing so.

Often, there are legitimate reasons to have a news conference. For example, you're probably more likely to get a story printed in the paper if there's a news conference (as opposed to just sending a media release).

On some races I've managed, if you sent out a media release, nobody would cover it. But if you held a news conference, five TV cameras would show up. On other races, a media release might generate a news story.

Lesson learned: Sometimes the media will only cover your story if you conduct a news conference.

But there *are* problems with news conferences. Unlike a well-scripted press release, after the candidate reads a prepared text at a news conference, he's subjected to answering questions about "anything."

That's why I strongly suggest prepping your candidate. If you're a serious candidate, you ought to bring in some folks to pepper you with tough questions on a regular basis. It's better to practice answering tough questions *before* you face the media.

Events That Warrant News Events

The following events are the kind of events that you should be looking for when it comes to holding a news conference.

- Your candidate's announcement
- To comment on the "local" angle of a national news story
- To point out deficiencies in your opponent's record
- To announce endorsements of prominent officials.
- Most importantly, to advance YOUR AGENDA and MESSAGE.

Please note that anytime you decide to hold an event to attack your opponent, make sure the accusations are true – that you're not also guilty of those accusations – and make sure you know *why* the opponent did what he did (was there a good reason for his actions?). As Joe Gaylord says, "If you have political dynamite to throw at your opponent, make sure that stick of dynamite is not shaped like a boomerang."

Assuming you decide it's a good idea to have a news event, following are a few quick tips that will make your life a whole lot easier:

Be a Gracious Host

I recommend providing coffee and donuts to reporters at your events. It may not sound like much, but like anything in life, the little gestures mean a lot. If you provide coffee and donuts, but your opponent doesn't, that subconsciously underlines the fact that you care about the reporter. And it could be the difference between a happy reporter and an angry reporter.

When It Comes To Events... (Room) Size Matters

In his excellent book, *The Advance Man*, former Kennedy advance man, Jerry Bruno gives advice *every* candidate should consider *before* they book an event location:

> *Remember the first rule of crowds: 25,000 people in a 50,000-seat stadium is a half-empty turnout. But 4,000 people in a hall that seats 3,000 is an overflow crowd. And it works that way on a crowd. People want the sense of being somewhere special, somewhere a lot of people are trying to get to. It depresses people to see empty seats all around them, makes them feel they've*

been conned into turning out for an event that wasn't all that special.

Lesson learned: Always book a location that's smaller than you need. And be prepared to deal with the whining of people who think you should hold your event at Madison Square Garden.

"Standing Ovation" Speeches

Some speeches are so powerful they generate immediate audience response. I've heard that John F. Kennedy's famous Berlin speech was so powerful that people physically began trying to tear down the wall.

Most likely, the speeches you and I give will generate slightly less enthusiasm. Nevertheless, we can also give "standing-ovation" speeches.

Franklin Roosevelt said, "In politics, nothing happens by accident. If it happens, you can bet it was planned that way." The best way to make sure you get a standing ovation is to plan for it.

Every time you give a speech, have four or five supporters scattered throughout the crowd. (It's important that they are in different parts of the room.) Tell these supporters that during a particular part of the speech they are to rise to their feet and begin clapping. People take their cues from others – it's human nature. If four people stand up and start applauding, the audience *will* follow, and you'll get a reputation as a "standing ovation" speaker.

Can I Get Back to You?

During a news event, reporters have an opportunity to ask you questions. If a reporter asks you a question you don't know the answer to, don't make up an answer or lie to them. Just say, "Let me check into that and get back to you later today." Then, you must follow through. Unless the question is: "Why are you running" there is no shame attached to saying, "Can I get back to you."

I Wear my Sunglasses…

Candidates should not wear sunglasses during parades, door-to-door, or press events. Any pictures taken of a candidate with sunglasses on are virtually useless because you have a candidate/elected official looking like a mob boss rather than a human being. Ever notice that on that fateful day in Dallas, the sun was shining bright, but JFK wasn't wearing sunglasses? "The eyes are the window to the soul" so the saying goes...if you're hiding your eyes, I feel as though you are hiding something from me.

Set the Stage

Regardless of how you look, audiences will also judge you based on what the stage looks like. From a public relations perspective, you should consider that any pictures taken of you during a speech would include visuals of the people and props behind (and beside) you.

For this reason, signs, flags, and other visual props are a good idea.

Too many candidates worry about what they're going to say and how they're going to dress for a news conference, but fail to pay any attention at all to the "stage" they're going to be on. This is a mistake because the background says a lot about who you are as a candidate.

When you hold a news conference, it's possible that not a lot of people will show up. You may be tempted to have your supporters in front of the candidate (as if they were listening to him). Instead, you should have your supporters behind the candidate. That way they will be in the picture.

In 2002, I helped Maryland State Senator Alex Mooney during his reelection. One of the things we were very aggressive about was making sure our visuals sent the right message to the voters.

In fact, we were so aggressive that when Congressman Bob Ehrlich visited Senator Mooney's district to campaign for Governor, we turned it into a Mooney for Senate rally.

Senator Alex Mooney (left) *at a rally for candidate* ***Bob Ehrlich (right)****. This wasn't a Mooney rally, but notice all the "Win with Mooney" signs behind them.*

The above picture was cropped and published on the front page of *The Frederick News Post*. Senator Alex Mooney (left) was cropped out because the story was about Rep. Ehrlich visiting Frederick. But because our staff was so aggressive, our signs were in the paper (behind the very popular Rep. Bob Ehrlich).

Send the Right Message

If you decide to have supporters stand behind you, make sure the people standing behind you are *credibl*e on the issue you're addressing. For example, if you were talking about social security, it would certainly be nice to have at least a few senior citizens in the audience behind you. The following Howard Kurtz article illustrates this point. It's in reference to George W. Bush's signing a ban on partial birth abortions. The article appeared in *The Washington Post*, November 10, 2003:

> *For a White House that very carefully arranges presidential backdrops (see also: "Mission Accomplished"), the Bush advance team appeared to fall down on the job Wednesday when President Bush was photographed signing the "partial birth" abortion ban surrounded by nothing but a bunch of men in suits. Democrats quickly noted that this was tantamount to signing a piece of immigration legislation without a single Hispanic participating. House Minority Leader Nancy Pelosi (D- Calif.) said she found the picture -- "of a group of men celebrating depriving women of a medical procedure that could save their health and their lives" -- "disconcerting." White House spokeswoman Claire Buchan said there were many women in the audience who happily would have joined the signing ceremony. But the ceremony was limited only to the legislation's co-sponsors, she said, and those all happened to be men in suits.*

As you can imagine, this was a public relations nightmare because it played into the stereotype that conservative men are trying to impose their will on women. The fact that several female lawmakers attended the event in the audience is irrelevant. What appeared on the front page of every paper in the nation was the picture of the stage. And perception is reality.

Chapter Seven Lessons

Coffee and Donuts Go a Long Way

Media Releases and News Events

- The first thing to think about when considering holding a press event is: Do I really need to have the event?

- Before holding a press event, make sure to prep the candidate with expected questions.

- Always book a location that's smaller than you need.

- If you want to be a "standing-ovation" speaker, you have to make it happen. Just have supporters rise to their feet and start clapping. Others in the audience will follow.

- Keep in mind that the stage behind you is just as important as how you look and what you say.

CONCLUSION

Run an Honorable Campaign

We must picture Hell as a state where everyone is perpetually concerned about his own dignity and advancement, where everyone has a grievance, and where everyone lives the deadly serious passions of envy, self-importance, and resentment.
- C.S. Lewis

This book was written to equip conservatives to do a better job of communications. Active participation in political campaigns is an important part of a healthy democracy. One of the best ways to participate is to become a good communicator. To achieve that, I suggest re-reading this book and attending as many political-training courses as possible.

As a leader, I also want to encourage you to run a vigorous and honorable campaign. And don't forget to be gracious in victory and in defeat. Like a great football coach, give credit to "the team" when things go right, and take the blame when things go wrong.

Remember, the worst impression you can ever give the media – or voters – is that you're power hungry and/or a sore loser. Politics is a long ballgame. Even if you lose this election, you never know when you might want to run for office again. Campaigns are emotional. That's why you must always strive to be gracious. *Ronald Reagan was a tough campaigner, but he always conducted himself with dignity. You and I should strive for the same.*

Lastly, as I've studied Ronald Reagan and other great communicators, I also want to encourage you to find some mentors of your own to study. Being a great communicator is a journey. May this book help you toward your journey of making America a better and stronger nation. I wish you the best of luck!

Teaching Elephants to Talk Tips

Want to Learn More???

- Give *Teaching Elephants to Talk* out to your Republican club or friends! For info regarding special bulk price breaks, email: Trainers@CampaignLeadership.com.

- Bring Matt's top-notch communications training to *your hometown*. For more info about Matt's training, go to www.CampaignLeadership.com.

- Sign up for Matt's weekly campaign tips, "Teaching Elephants to Talk Tips." You can register online at www.CampaignLeadership.com.

- Read Matt's daily blog at www.MattLewis.org.

Teaching Elephants to Talk

About the Author:

Matt Lewis is President of The Campaign Leadership Company (www.CampaignLeadership.com). He has managed campaigns ranging from School Board to U.S. Congress, in states ranging from Maryland to North Dakota. In 2002, *Campaigns & Elections Magazine* named him a "Rising Star of Politics." Email Matt at MLewis@CampaignLeadership.com.